12 WEEK MARINE CORPS RECRUIT TRAINING

Josh Honsberger and Nick Koumalatsos

DISCLAIMERS

The material and information in this Ebook are for general informational purposes only and are provided "as is" and without warranties of any kind, either expressed or implied. Alexander Industries LLC disclaims any and all warranties, including but not limited to implied warranties
of merchantability and fitness for a particular purpose.

Any fitness or exercise training program contains inherent risks of physical injury or death. This Ebook is not intended to be a substitute for the medical advice of a licensed physician. You should consult your physician before beginning any new exercise program.

www.usmcprep.com
www.alexanderind.com
USMCPREP Videos

TABLE OF CONTENTS

12 WEEK MARINE CORPS

BASIC TRAINING PREP

BLUF (BOTTOM LINE UP FRONT)

This is a 12-week program designed to develop the strength and stamina to successfully complete every physical aspect of Marine Corps Basic Training. The overall goal of this program is to max out the PFT, CFT, and Swim Qualification. While having overall stamina to be physically superior while attending Marine Corps Basic Training. We have scientifically broken down this training to get you to optimize your potential without over training or causing injury. It requires output, consistency, and outcome is dependent on your efforts.

PHYSICAL TRAINING DESCRIPTION

This program is a progressive and intense 6 day per week training regimen. Ideally you will train Monday through Saturday, and take Sunday as full rest day. If for some reason you cannot keep this schedule, do not skip any sessions, do them exactly in order as they are designed. The reason for this is to prepare you for the rigors of training everyday except Sundays while you are in basic training.

Your program will be split into three 3 week cycles, with a de-load week in between them. Programing will progress each week and become more difficult. The purpose of this ramp up style is to establish a solid foundation to build upon as well as ensure you are free from injury. Remember the whole goal of this is to gain the skills you need to become a United States Marine.

If you start your training on a Monday then here is what your week will look like:

Monday:	**Strength**
Tuesday:	Stamina
Wednesday:	Strength
Thursday:	Pool PT
Friday:	Strength
Saturday:	Active Recovery

Sunday:	Recovery

As much as we need to build discipline and stick to a routine, we understand that life happens. If for some reason you miss a day, start with the training session you missed and stick to the training schedule.

Your training program can be completed in any gym with the use of a few dumbbells, barbell, and plates. As programing progresses, the workouts will become more intense and difficult.

RECOMMENDED GEAR LIST

- ✓ TRX (USE: USMCTRX for 20% off site wide)
- ✓ Dumbbells
- ✓ Kettlebells
- ✓ Resistance Bands (can get at TRX)
- ✓ Pair of camouflage utilities (go to an old surplus store, nothing special, not pattern specific)

EXERCISE TUTORIALS

Exercise tutorials can be found on Nick Koumalatsos Youtube page under the USMC PREP Playlist. www.youtube.com/c/nickoumalatsos

DIET

We have all heard the term "trash in, trash out". This is 100% true. The goal of this training is to get you to 100% of your maximum capability prior to going to Basic Training. Once you get to Paris Island or San Diego you will not have control of your environment. So let's start acting like a Marine now and be prepared for the mission at hand. You have control of your current environment which gives us an advantage in our training.

Why do race cars only use high octane fuel? Because they want to perform the best that they can. Our bodies are the same way! If we expect our bodies to perform like the Best Of The Best, the Few and The Proud, then we need to fuel it accordingly.

We STRONGLY recommend only eating foods that can be grown or killed. Marines say "Blood makes the grass grow", well it also makes you grow.

EAT	DON'T EAT
Meats (Grass fed Preferably)	Refined Sugar
Fish/Seafood	Cereal
Fresh Fruits	Processed Foods
Fresh Vegetables	Salty Foods
Eggs	Refined Vegetable Oils
Nuts	Candy/Junk/Soda
Seeds	
Healthy Oils	

This means your soda and ANY fast food is off the table! It is time to turn your body into a lean mean fighting machine and this is how we are going to do it.

On Saturday we want you to refeed. This means for ONE meal you will eat your meal of choice: Burger, Pizza, or whatever your favorite is. We always try to still eat real food. For instance we will go have a pizza at a local pizza joint using real ingredients. Not to a fast food joint to crush a fake burger and fries.

WATER CONSUMPTION

We recommend that you consume a minimum of 4 quarts of water a day. One of the most common cause for injury and casualties during basic training is either dehydration, heat exhaustion, or heat stroke. This can easily be combated by staying hydrated during the day. Start trying to drink water right before a training exercise and you are already 12 hours too late. You have to stay on top of it and stay in front of dehydration. This is something that your Drill Instructors will do their best to ensure. So with that thought in mind you need to get use to consuming that amount of water. Get a gallon jug and fill it up every morning or go and buy a canteen and drink 4 of them a day. This is the chart that you will see in many of the Marine Corps Heads.

Drink water, coffee, and tea - everything else is off limits!

SLEEP

Sleep could be the most crucial part of this program! When we sleep, our bodies release all the good hormones that help our body recovery and grow new muscle mass. It also helps with brain function and brain health. Have you ever spoken to someone after they have not slept for 3 days? They are not very coherent, are they?

The Marine Corps understands this, which is why there is such a strict schedule while in Basic Training. While in Marine Corps Basic Training you will receive 8 hours of scheduled sleep. Minus the hour you have fire watch (if you are on schedule).

For the same reason, we want you to implement the same sleep schedule to prepare yourself for this part of Basic Training. The whole point is to be 100% prepared for this environment. By implementing this sleep regime, showing up to Basic Training will not be such a shock. However, we understand your work/school commitments and ask for you to do the very best that you can based on your circumstance.

The overall goal is a minimum of 8 hours of sleep. But because we are Marines and soon to be Marines we are going to take it a step further. Whatever your normal wake up time is, you are going to start by waking up 2 hours earlier until you get to 0500. For instance if you are use to waking up at 9am your protocol will look as such:

- ***Week 1: 0700 Reveille - NLT (No Later Than) 2300 Lights Out***

- ***Week 2: 0600 Reveille - NLT 2200 Lights Out***

- ***Week 3: 0500 Reveille - NLT 2100 Lights Out***

We understand that life happens and you should enjoy your life prior to Basic Training. If you slack off for a night just reset and get right back on the program.

THIS SLEEP PROTOCOL IS JUST AS IMPORTANT AS THE TRAINING! DO NOT GAFF IT OFF!

MARINE CORPS REQUIREMENTS

Here are the latest Standards for each graded Marine Corps Exercise. As well as the Marine Corps PFT (Physical Fitness Test) and CFT (Combat Fitness Test)

Prior to beginning the 12 week USMC Prep protocol you will need to perform a PFT & CFT in order to establish a starting point and a comparison for the completion of the USMC Prep program. Annotate your reps, time and scores below for the given exercises and overall scores. The Marine Corps standards are as follows.

PFT

Crunches - regardless of age crunch reps/points will be assessed and awarded based on the 17-20 age bracket. Below is listed as Reps and under is the points awarded for the reps.

105	104	103	102	101	100	99	98	97	96	95	94	93	92	91	90	89	88	87	86
100	98	97	95	93	91	90	88	86	85	83	81	79	78	76	74	73	71	69	67

85	84	83	82	81	80	79	78	77	76	75	74	73	72	71	70
66	64	62	61	59	57	55	54	52	50	49	47	45	43	42	40

Pull Ups - regardless of age pull-ups reps/points will be assessed and awarded based on the 17-20 age bracket. Below is listed as Reps and under is the points awarded for the reps.

20	19	18	17	16	15	14	13	12	11	10	9	8	7	6	5	4
100	96	93	89	85	81	78	74	70	66	63	59	55	51	48	44	40

Push Ups - regardless of age push-ups reps/points will be assessed and awarded based on the 17-20 age bracket. Below is listed as Reps and under is the points awarded for the reps.

82	81	80	79	78	77	76	75	74	73	72	71	70	69	68	67	66	65	64	63
70	69	69	68	67	66	66	65	64	63	63	62	61	60	60	59	58	57	57	56

62	61	60	59	58	57	56	55	54	53	52	51	50	49	48	47	46	45	44	43
55	54	54	53	52	51	51	50	49	48	48	47	46	45	45	44	43	42	42	41

3 mile run - regardless of age the 3 mile run time/points will be assessed and awarded based on the 17-20 age bracket. Below is listed as Time and under is the points awarded for the time.

7	18:10	18:20	18:30	18:40	18:50	19:00	19:10	19:20	19:30	19:40	19:50	20:00	20:10	20:20	20:30	20:40
100	99	98	97	96	95	94	93	92	91	90	89	88	87	86	84	83

20:50	21:00	21:10	21:20	21:30	21:40	21:50	22:00	22:10	22:20	22:30	22:40	22:50	23:00	23:10	23:20	23:30
82	81	80	79	78	77	76	75	74	73	72	71	70	69	68	67	66

This is a MAX effort event for all prescribed components! Leave nothing in the tank. This will get a real full picture as to where you are sitting.

PFT	QTY. / TIME	POINTS
CRUNCHES	105/2:28	100
PULL-UPS	6 (36 Push-ups)	48
3 MILE RUN	23:00	69

PFT SCORE - 217

CFT

Ammo Can Lift(ACL) - regardless of age ACL reps/points will be assessed and awarded based on the 17-20 age bracket. Below is listed as Reps and under is the points awarded for the reps.

106	105	104	103	102	101	100	99	98	97	96	95	94	93	92	91	90	89	88	87
100	99	97	96	95	93	92	90	89	88	86	85	84	82	81	80	78	77	75	74

86	85	84	83	82	81	80	79	78	77	76	75	74	73	72	71	70	69	68	67
73	71	70	69	67	66	65	63	62	60	59	58	56	55	54	52	51	50	48	47

Movement to Contact (MTC) - regardless of age the MTC time/points will be assessed and awarded based on the 17-20 age bracket. Below is listed as Time and under is the points awarded for the time.

2:4	2:4	2:4	2:4	2:4	2:4	2:4	2:4	2:4	2:4	2:5	2:5	2:5	2:5	2:5	2:5	2:5	2:5	2:5	2:5
100	99	98	97	96	95	94	94	93	92	91	90	89	88	87	86	85	84	83	82

3:00	3:01	3:02	3:03	3:04	3:05	3:06	3:07	3:08	3:09	3:10	3:11	3:12	3:13	3:14	3:15	3:16	3:17	3:18	3:19
82	81	80	79	78	77	76	75	74	73	72	71	70	70	69	68	67	66	65	64

Maneuver Under (MANUF) - regardless of age the MTC time/points will be assessed and awarded based on the 17-20 age bracket. Below is listed as Time and under is the points awarded for the time.

2:0	2:0	2:0	2:1	2:1	2:1	2:1	2:1	2:1	2:1	2:1	2:1	2:1	2:2	2:2	2:2	2:2	2:2	2:2	2:2

100	99	98	97	97	96	95	94	93	92	91	91	90	89	88	87	86	85	85	84

2:2	2:2	2:2	2:3	2:3	2:3	2:3	2:3	2:3	2:3	2:3	2:3	2:3	2:4	2:4	2:4	2:4	2:4	2:4	2:4
83	82	81	80	79	79	78	77	76	75	74	73	73	72	71	70	69	68	67	67

This is a MAX effort event for all prescribed components! Leave nothing in the tank. This will get a real full picture as to where you are sitting.

CFT	QTY. / TIME	POINTS
AMMO CAN LIFT (ACL)		
MOVEMENT TO CONTACT (MTC)		
MANEUVER UNDER FIRE (MANUF)		

CFT SCORE -

WARM UP PROTOCOL

Prior to EVERY training session perform the warm up protocol as prescribed below. This includes active recovery days as well. You can perform this protocol on Sundays as well if desired. Do not slack off. Consistency throughout your training regime is crucial to you bodies development and success.

Part 1

- Foam Roll
- Jumping Jacks x10 - 4 count
- Straight Leg Band Walks (each way/band around ankles) x10m
- Half Squat Band Walks (each way/band above knee) x10m

Part 2

- 2 Rounds
- Bodyweight Squat x 10
- Walking Knee Hug x 10m
- Walking Quad Stretch x 10m
- Walking Leg Cradle x 10m
- Walk Toe Touch x 10m
- High Knees x 10m
- Butt Kicks x 10m

- Backpedal x 10m
- Lateral Shuffle x 10m
- Carioca x 10m

Part 3

- Band Pull Aparts Front x10
- Band Pull Aparts Overhead x10
- Y,T,I x5-10 each way
- Mountain Climber x10 4 count

COMMON ACRONYMS YOU WILL FIND THROUGHOUT THE TRAINING PROGRAM:

SA	**Single Arm**
DA	Double Arm
MB	Medicine Ball
BB	Barbell
RDS	Rounds
TRX	https://www.trxtraining.com/#/
DB	Dumbbell
SADB	Single Arm Dumbbell
DADB	Double Arm Dumbbell
KB	Kettlebell
DKB	Double Kettlebell
SAKB	Single Arm Kettlebell
DAKB	Double Arm Kettlebell

TRAINING PROGRAM

WEEK 1

SESSION 1

OBJECTIVE: STRENGTH

→ TRX Squat 3x15 -30sec rest between rds

→ DB Bench 3x15 - 30sec rest between rds

→ DB Push Press 3 X 15 -30sec rest between rds

Rest interval between each set of push-ups will be the amount of time in sec it took to perform 22 push-ups. Asses this time each week and adjust accordingly.

Push Ups	22	22	20	18	18	10

3RDS

- 20sec rest between exercises.
- TRX Hamstring Curl x 10
- TRX Pistol Squats x5 each leg
- Rest 60sec between rounds

3RDS

- 20sec rest between exercises
- TRX Bulgarian Split Squat x6 each leg
- TRX Side Plank x45 sec
- Wall Sit 3x30sec
- Rest 60sec between rounds

SESSION 2

OBJECTIVE: STAMINA

4 rounds

- Shuttle Sprints
- 5/10/5 meters down and back = 40m
- : 30-sec rest between rounds

4 rounds

- 60m Sprint
- : 30-sec rest between rounds

SESSION 3

OBJECTIVE: STRENGTH

- → DB Deadlift 3x15 -30-sec rest between rds
- → 4 count Flutter kicks 3x10
- → Lat Pull-Down 3x15 -30-sec rest between rds
- → TRX Inverted Row 3x15 -30-sec rest between rds

Pull Ups should be performed in accordance with USMC standards. If you are unable to perform the prescribed pull-ups, the remainder can be assisted with bands. Rest interval should be equal to the amount of time it takes to perform the first set of pull-ups. Perform each rep as quickly and as explosively as possible.

Pull Ups	6	6	6	5	4
Rest					

3RDS

- 20sec rest between exercises
- TRX Bicep Curl x15
- TRX Tricep Curl x15
- TRX Glute Bridge w/ Curl x15
- Rest 60sec between rounds

Crunches should be performed to USMC standards. Crunches should be performed explosively, rest interval between each set will` be equal to the time it takes to perform the first set of crunches. Rest interval should be assessed each week and adjusted as needed.

Crunches	35	35	35	35	35

SESSION 4

OBJECTIVE: POOL PT

- Stroke refinement and skillsacquisition
- Performed wearing Swim Trunks
- Rest iteration between prescribed tasks are to be no more than 5 mins.

Swim sessions should always be performed in the presence of a lifeguard or another individual who is able to provide assistance if necessary.

- Side Stroke Left Side - 4x25m
- Side Stroke Right Side - 4x25m
- Breast Stroke - 4x25m
- Underwater Crossover - 5x10m
- Tread Water - 3x 5mins

SESSION 5

OBJECTIVE: STRENGTH

- → TRX Squat Single Leg -3x6each leg -30-sec rest between rds
- → DB Floor Press-3x15 -30-sec rest between rds
- → TRX High Row (Face Pull)-3x15 -30-sec rest between rds

Crunches should be performed to USMC standards. Crunches should be performed explosively, rest interval between each set will be equal to the time it takes to perform the first set of crunches. Rest interval should be assessed each week and adjusted as needed.

Crunches	35	35	35	35	35

3RDS

- 20sec rest between exercises
- TRX Alternating Lateral Lunge-3x6 each leg
- Band Rotations - 3x15
- TRX Plank to Side Crunch-3x6 each side
- Rest 60sec between rounds

Shuttle Sprints

- 4 rounds
- : 20-sec rest between rounds
- 10M-Down & Back x6= 120m

SESSION 6

OBJECTIVE: ACTIVE RECOVERY DAYS:

1 Hour Sustained Activity. You can Hike, Run, Swim, Bike, Row or Play Football, Rugby, Soccer, Basketball. Any activity of your choice where you have sustained movement for a minimum of 1 hour.

Record Steps/Distance each week.

WEEK 2

SESSION 7

OBJECTIVE: STRENGTH

- → Goblet Squats - 4x12 - 30sec rest between rds
- → DB Bench - 4x12 - 30sec rest between rds
- → Seated DB military Press- 4x12 - 30sec rest between rds

Push Ups should be performed to USMC standards.
Rest interval between each set of push ups will be the amount of time in sec it took to perform 22 push ups. Asses this time each week and adjust accordingly.

Push Ups	22	22	20	18	18	8	6

4x12

- 20sec rest between exercises
- TRX Hamstring Curl
- Leg Extension
- TRX Explosive Squats
- 60 sec rest between rounds
- SA Farmers Carry(left arm) x50m
- Front Plank x :60sec
- SA Farmers Carry(right arm) x50m
- Left Plank x :60sec
- SA Farmers Carry(left arm) x50m
- Right Plank x :60sec
- SA Farmers Carry(right arm) x50m
- Front Plank x :60sec

SESSION 8

OBJECTIVE: STAMINA

4 rounds

- Shuttle Sprints
- 5/10/5 meters down and back = 40m
- : 30-sec rest between rounds

4 rounds

- 60m Sprint
- : 45-sec rest between rounds

SESSION 9

OBJECTIVE: STRENGTH

- → **KB Swing - 4x12 - 30sec rest between rds**
- → **Lat Pull-Down- 4x12 - 30sec rest between rds**
- → **TRX inverted row 4x12 - 30sec rest between rds**

Pull Ups Should be performed in accordance with USMC standards. If you are unable to perform the prescribed pull ups, the remainder can be assisted with bands.

Rest interval should be equal to the amount of time it takes to perform the first set of pullups. Perform each rep as quickly and as explosively as possible.

Pull Ups	7	6	5	4	4	4

4x12

- 20 sec rest between exercises
- DB RDL x10
- TRX Bicep Curl x12
- 60 sec rest between rounds

4x12

- 20 sec rest between exercises
- TRX Tricep Extension x12
- TRX Explosive Glute Bridge with hello dolly x 10
- 60 sec rest between rounds

Crunches should be performed to USMC standards. Crunches should be performed explosively, rest interval between each set will be equal to the time it takes to perform the first set of crunches

Rest interval should be assessed each week and adjusted as needed.

Crunches	35	35	35	35	35
Rest					

SESSION 10

OBJECTIVE: POOL PT

Push Ups should be performed to USMC standards.

Rest interval between each set of push-ups will be the amount of time in sec it took to perform 22 push-ups. Assess this time each week and adjust accordingly.

Push Ups	22	22	20	18	18	8	6

Stroke refinement and skills acquisition Performed wearing Swim Trunks

Rest iteration between prescribed tasks are to be no more than 5 mins.

Swim sessions should always be performed in the presence of a lifeguard or another individual who is able to provide assistance if necessary.

- Side Stroke Left Side - 4x25m
- Side Stroke Right Side - 4x25m
- Breast Stroke - 4x25m
- Underwater Crossover - 5x10m
- Tread Water - 3x 5mins

SESSION 11

OBJECTIVE: STRENGTH

- → Walking Lunges - 4x10 - 30sec rest between rds
- → BB Floor Press- 4x12 - 30sec rest between rds
- → BB Bent Over Row- 4x12 - 30sec rest between rds

4x12

- 20 sec rest between exercises
- Band Chest Fly (explosive)
- Band Retractions
- 60 sec rest between rounds

4x12

- 20 sec rest between exercises
- TRX Jump Split Squat
- Band Rotations
- 60 sec rest between rounds

Shuttle Sprints

- 4 rounds
- 15M-Down & Back x6= 180m

SESSION 12

OBJECTIVE: ACTIVE RECOVERY DAYS

1 Hour Sustained Activity. You can Hike, Run, Swim, Bike, Row or Play Football, Rugby, Soccer, Basketball. Any activity of your choice where you have sustained movement for a minimum of 1 hour.

Record Steps/Distance each week.

WEEK 3

SESSION 13

OBJECTIVE: STRENGTH

Shuttle Run

- 4 rounds
- 5/10/20 Down & Back = 70m
- : 30-sec rest

→ Goblet Squat - 4x12 - 30sec rest between rds

→ TRX Explosive Squats 4x6 30sec rest between rds

→ DB Bench - 4x12 - 30sec rest between rds

→ DB Push Press - 4x12 - 30sec rest between rds

Push Ups should be performed to USMC standards.

Rest interval between each set of push-ups will be the amount of time in sec it took to perform 22 push-ups. Assess this time each week and adjust accordingly.

Push Ups	22	22	20	18	18	10	10

Crunches should be performed to USMC standards. Crunches should be performed explosively, rest interval between each set will be equal to the time it takes to perform the first set of crunches. Rest interval should be assessed each week and adjusted as needed.

Crunches	35	35	35	35	35

4x12

- 20 sec rest between exercises
- Squat Jump
- Plate Curl to Press
- 60 sec rest between rounds

→ SA Farmers Carry(left arm) x50m

→ Front Plank x :60sec

→ SA Farmers Carry(right arm) x50m

→ Left Plank x :60sec

→ SA Farmers Carry(left arm) x50m

→ Right Plank x :60sec

→ SA Farmers Carry(right arm) x50m

→ Front Plank x :60sec

SESSION 14

OBJECTIVE: STAMINA

These sprints are designed to be max effort sprints. Your rest interval is going to be the average of the time it took you to run your first two 300m sprints. That rest interval will be the same for EVERY sprint. Your rest is a rest in motion, keep the body erect and moving.

If your times begin to vary more than 10%, you need to take additional rest in order to get your timing back within the 10%. However do not exceed the rest interval if not necessary, it is key to progress!

Distance	300m	300m	300m	300m
Time				

Distance	200m	200m	200m	200m	200m	200m	200m	200m

Time								

Distance	100m	100m	100m	100m	100m	100m	100m	100m
Time								

SESSION 15

OBJECTIVE: STRENGTH

- → **DB Deadlift - 4x12 - 30sec rest between rds**
- → **Band Pull throughs 4x6 30sec rest between rds**
- → **Banded Pulldowns - 4x12 - 30sec rest between rds**
- → **TRX Inverted Row - 4x12 - 30sec rest between rds**

Pull Ups Should be performed in accordance with USMC standards. If you are unable to perform the prescribed pull ups, the remainder can be assisted with bands.

Rest interval should be equal to the amount of time it takes to perform the first set of pullups. Perform each rep as quickly and as explosively as possible.

Pull Ups	8	7	6	4	4	4

Crunches should be performed to USMC standards. Crunches should be performed explosively, rest interval between each set will be equal to the time it takes to perform the first set of crunches. Rest interval should be assessed each week and adjusted as needed.

Crunches	35	35	35	35	35

4x12

- :20 sec rest between exercises
- DB Front raise
- DB side raise

4x12

- :20 sec rest between exercises
- DB Hammer Curls each arm
- 4 count flutter kicks

SESSION 16

OBJECTIVE: POOL PT

Push Ups should be performed to USMC standards.

Rest interval between each set of push-ups will be the amount of time in sec it took to perform 22 push-ups.

Assess this time each week and adjust accordingly.

Push Ups	22	22	20	18	18	10	10

Stroke refinement and skills acquisition

Some iterations will be performed wearing Swim Trunks and some with cammie tops & bottoms. Ensure you check the prescribed attire.

Rest iteration between prescribed tasks are to be no more than 5 mins.

Swim sessions should always be performed in the presence of a lifeguard or another individual who is able to provide assistance if necessary.

Swim Trunks

- Side Stroke Left Side - 4x25m
- Side Stroke Right Side - 4x25m
- Breast Stroke - 4x25m

Cammie Bottoms

- Side Stroke Left Side - 2x25m
- Side Stroke Right Side - 2x25m
- Breast Stroke - 2x25m

Underwater Crossover

- Cammie Bottoms - 3x10m
- Swim Trunks - 2x15m

Tread Water

- Cammie Bottoms - 2x 5 mins
- Swim Trunks - 2x 10 mins

SESSION 17

OBJECTIVE: STRENGTH

- → **Step up w/DB & Step Down- 4x12 - 30sec rest between rds**
- → **DB Floor Press- 4x12 - 30sec rest between rds**
- → **Banded Bent Over Rows - 4x12 - 30sec Rest between rds**

Pull Ups Should be performed in accordance with USMC standards. If you are unable to perform the prescribed pull ups, the remainder can be assisted with bands. Rest interval should be equal to the amount of time it takes to perform the first set of pullups. Perform each rep as quickly and as explosively as possible.

Pull Ups	8	7	6	4	4	4

Crunches should be performed to USMC standards. Crunches should be performed explosively, rest interval between each set will be equal to the time it takes to perform the first set of crunches. Rest interval should be assessed each week and adjusted as needed.

Crunches	35	35	35	35	35

4x12

- 20 sec rest between exercises
- DB Incline Press
- Hang Explosive Knee Raise
- Rest 45 sec between rounds

4x12

- 20 sec rest between exercises
- DB Tricep Extension
- MB Hip Toss 6 each side
- Rest 45 sec between rounds

4 rounds

- 15M-Down & Back x6= 180m
- 1:00 rest

SESSION 18

OBJECTIVE: ACTIVE RECOVERY DAYS:

1 Hour Sustained Activity. You can Hike, Run, Swim, Bike, Row or Play Football, Rugby, Soccer, Basketball. Any activity of your choice where you have sustained movement for a minimum of 1 hour.

Record Steps/Distance each week.

WEEK 4

SESSION 19

OBJECTIVE: STRENGTH

Shuttle Run

- 5 rounds
- 5/10/20 Down & Back
- : 30-sec rest

→ Goblet Squat - 4x15 - 30sec rest between rds

→ DB Bench Press - 4x15 - 30sec rest between rds

→ Seated Arnold Press - 4x15 - 30sec rest between rds

Push Ups should be performed to USMC standards.

Rest interval between each set of push-ups will be the amount of time in sec it took to perform 22 push-ups. Asses this time each week and adjust accordingly.

Push Up	22	22	20	18	18	10	8	8

Crunches should be performed to USMC standards. Crunches should be performed explosively, rest interval between each set will be equal to the time it takes to perform the first set of crunches. Rest interval should be assessed each week and adjusted as needed.

Crunches	35	35	35	35	35

4x10

- 20 sec est between exercises
- TRX Explosive Squats
- Cuban Press
- TRX Oblique Crunch
- Rest 60 sec between rounds

SESSION 20

OBJECTIVE: STAMINA

These sprints are designed to be max effort sprints. Your rest interval is going to be the average of the time it took you to run your first two 300m sprints. That rest interval will be the same for EVERY sprint. Your rest is a rest in motion, keep the body erect and moving.

If your times begin to vary more than 10%, you need to take additional rest in order to get your timing back within the 10%. However, do not exceed the rest interval if not necessary, it is key to progress!

Distance	300m	300m	300m	300m
Time				

Distance	200m	200m	200m	200m	200m	200m	200m	200m

Time								

Distance	100m	100m	100m	100m	100m	100m	100m	100m
Time								

SESSION 21

OBJECTIVE: STRENGTH

- → **DB Deadlift - 4x15 - 30sec rest between rds**
- → **Band Pull throughs - 4x15 - 30sec rest between rds**
- → **Lat Pull Downs - 4x15 - 30sec rest between rds**

Pull Ups should be performed in accordance with USMC standards. If you are unable to perform the prescribed pull-ups, the remainder can be assisted with bands. Rest interval should be equal to the amount of time it takes to perform the first set of pull-ups. Perform each rep as quickly and as explosively as possible.

Pull Ups	9	8	6	4	3	3

4x10

- 20 sec rest between exercises
- Chest Supported DB Row
- Explosive Plank to Squat
- Rest 45 sec between rounds

4x10

- 20 sec rest between exercises
- Renegade Row
- TRX Pike
- Rest 60 sec between rounds

SESSION 22

OBJECTIVE: POOL PT

Push Ups should be performed to USMC standards.

Rest interval between each set of push ups will be the amount of time in sec it took to perform 22 push ups. Asses this time each week and adjust accordingly.

Push Up	22	22	20	18	18	10	8	8

Stroke refinement and skills acquisition

Some iterations will be performed wearing Swim Trunks and some with cammie tops & bottoms. Ensure you check the prescribed attire.

Rest iteration between prescribed tasks are to be no more than 5 mins.

Swim sessions should always be performed in the presence of a lifeguard or another individual who is able to provide assistance if necessary.

Swim Trunks

- Side Stroke Left Side - 4x25m
- Side Stroke Right Side - 4x25m
- Breast Stroke - 4x25m

Cammie Bottoms

- Side Stroke Left Side - 2x25m
- Side Stroke Right Side - 2x25m
- Breast Stroke - 2x25m

Underwater Crossover

- Cammie Bottoms - 3x10m
- Swim Trunks - 2x15m

Tread Water

- Cammie Bottoms - 2x 5 mins
- Swim Trunks - 2x 10 mins

SESSION 23

OBJECTIVE: STRENGTH

4 rounds

- **15M-Down & Back x6= 180m**
- **1:30 rest**

→ **TRX Alternating Lunges - 4x7 each leg - 30sec rest between rds**

→ **DB Floor Press - 4x15 - 30sec rest between rds**

→ **Single Arm DB Row - 4x15 - 30sec rest between rds**

Pull Ups should be performed in accordance with USMC standards. If you are unable to perform the prescribed pull-ups, the remainder can be assisted with bands. Rest interval should be equal to the amount of time it takes to perform the first set of pull-ups. Perform each rep as quickly and as explosively as possible.

Pull Ups	9	8	6	4	3	3

Crunches should be performed to USMC standards. Crunches should be performed explosively, rest interval between each set will be equal to the time it takes to perform the first set of crunches. Rest interval should be assessed each week and adjusted as needed

Crunches	35	35	35	35	35

4x10

- 20 sec rest between exercises
- TRX Jump Lunges
- Band Rotations
- MB Side Throw
- Rest 60 sec between rounds

4x10

- 20 sec est between exercises
- TRX Alternating Lateral Lunges
- Bar Hang Knee Raises
- MB Slams
- Rest 60 sec between rounds

SESSION 24

OBJECTIVE: ACTIVE RECOVERY DAYS:

1 Hour Sustained Activity. You can Hike, Run, Swim, Bike, Row or Play Football, Rugby, Soccer, Basketball. Any activity of your choice where you have sustained movement for a minimum of 1 hour.

Record Steps/Distance each week.

WEEK 5

SESSION 25

OBJECTIVE: STRENGTH

Shuttle Run

- 4 rounds
- 10/20/30 Down & Back
- : 45-sec rest

→ DKB Rack Squat - 3x10 - 90 sec Rest Between RDS

→ DB Bench - 3x10 - 90 sec Rest Between RDS

→ DB Chest Push Press - 3x10 - 90 sec Rest Between RDS

Push Ups should be performed to USMC standards.

Rest interval between each set of push-ups will be the amount of time in sec it took to perform 22 push-ups. Assess this time each week and adjust accordingly.

Push Up	22	22	20	18	18	10	10	10

3x12

- 20 sec rest between exercises
- TRX Bulgarian Split Squat
- Plate Curl to Press
- Rest 45 sec between rounds

3x12

- 20 rest between exercises
- TRX Pistol Squats
- Bar Dead Hang - MAX Time
- Rest 60 sec between rounds

Crunches should be performed to USMC standards. Crunches should be performed explosively, rest interval between each set will be equal to the time it takes to perform the first set of crunches. Rest interval should be assessed each week and adjusted as needed.

Crunches	35	35	35	35	35

SESSION 26

OBJECTIVE: STAMINA

These sprints are designed to be max effort sprints. Your rest interval is going to be the average of the time it took you to run your first two 300m sprints. That rest interval will be the same for EVERY sprint. Your rest is a rest in motion, keep the body erect and moving.

If your times begin to vary more than 10%, you need to take additional rest in order to get your timing back within the 10%. However do not exceed the rest interval if not necessary, it is key to progress!

Distance	300m	300m	300m	300m
Time				

Distance	200m	200m	200m	200m	200m	200m	200m	200m	200m	200m

Time										

Distance	100m	100m	100m	100m	100m	100m	100m	100m
Time								

SESSION 27

OBJECTIVE: STRENGTH

- → **Deadlift - 3x10 - 90 sec Rest Between RDS**
- → **Band Retractions - 3x10 - 90 sec Rest Between RDS**
- → **DB Pullover- 3x10 - 90 sec Rest Between RDS**
- → **Chest Supported DB Row- 3x10 - 90 sec Rest Between RDS**

Pull Ups Should be performed in accordance with USMC standards. If you are unable to perform the prescribed pull ups, the remainder can be assisted with bands. Rest interval should be equal to the amount of time it takes to perform the first set of pullups. Perform each rep as quickly and as explosively as possible.

Pull Ups	10	8	6	5	3	3

3x12

- 20 sec rest between exercises
- Explosive Plank 2 Squat
- TRX Tricep Curl
- MB Slams
- Rest 60 sec between rounds

3x12

- 20 sec rest between exercises
- TRX Bicep Curl
- TRX Leg Curl
- Explosive Glute Bridge
- Rest 60 sec between rounds

→ Dead Bar Hang-MAX Tim

SESSION 28

OBJECTIVE: POOL PT

Push Ups should be performed to USMC standards.

Rest interval between each set of push ups will be the amount of time in sec it took to perform 22 push ups. Assess this time each week and adjust accordingly.

Push Up	22	22	20	18	18	10	10	10

Stroke refinement and skills acquisition

Some iterations will be performed wearing Swim Trunks and some with cammie tops & bottoms. Ensure you check the prescribed attire.

Rest iteration between prescribed tasks are to be no more than 5 mins.

Swim sessions should always be performed in the presence of a lifeguard or another individual who is able to provide assistance if necessary.

Swim Trunks

- Side Stroke Left Side - 4x25m
- Side Stroke Right Side - 4x25m
- Breast Stroke - 4x25m

Cammie Top & Bottoms

- Side Stroke Left Side - 2x25m
- Side Stroke Right Side - 2x25m
- Breast Stroke - 2x25m

Underwater Crossover

- Cammie Top & Bottoms - 3x10m
- Swim Trunks - 2x15m

Tread Water

- Cammie Top & Bottoms - 2x 5 mins
- Swim Trunks - 2x 10 mins

SESSION 29

OBJECTIVE: STRENGTH

4 rounds

- 20M-Down & Back x6= 240m
- 1:00 rest

→ DB walking lunges- 3x10 - 90 sec Rest Between RDS

→ Power step ups- 3x5 each leg - 90 sec Rest Between RDS

→ DB Floor Press- 3x10 - 90 sec Rest Between RDS

→ TRX Body Saw- 3x5 - 90 sec Rest Between RDS

→ SADB Row- 3x10 - 90 sec Rest Between RDS

Pull Ups Should be performed in accordance with USMC standards. If you are unable to perform the prescribed pull ups, the remainder can be assisted with bands. Rest interval should be equal to the amount of time it takes to perform the first set of pullups. Perform each rep as quickly and as explosively as possible.

Pull Ups	10	8	6	5	3	3

Crunches should be performed to USMC standards. Crunches should be performed explosively, rest interval between each set will be equal to the time it takes to perform the first set of crunches. Rest interval should be assessed each week and adjusted as needed.

Crunches	35	35	35	35	35

3x12

- 20 sec rest between exercises
- TRX Side Crunch
- KB Alt lateral Lunge
- Rest 45 sec between rounds

3x12

- 20 sec rest between exercises
- MB Side Throws
- Bar Hang knee raise
- Alternating Jump Lunge
- Rest 60 sec between rounds

SESSION 30

OBJECTIVE: ACTIVE RECOVERY DAYS:

1 Hour Sustained Activity. You can Hike, Run, Swim, Bike, Row or Play Football, Rugby, Soccer, Basketball. Any activity of your choice where you have sustained movement for a minimum of 1 hour.

Record Steps/Distance each week.

WEEK 6

SESSION 31

OBJECTIVE: STRENGTH

Shuttle Run

- 4 rounds
- 10/20/30 Down & Back
- : 45-sec rest

→ DKB Rack Squat - 4x10 - 90 sec Rest Between RDS

→ DB Incline Press - 4x10 - 90 sec Rest Between RDS

→ DB Chest Push Press - 4x10 - 90 sec Rest Between RDS

Push Ups should be performed to USMC standards.

Rest interval between each set of push ups will be the amount of time in sec it took to perform 22 push-ups. Assess this time each week and adjust accordingly.

Push Up	22	22	20	18	18	10	10	8	8

Crunches should be performed to USMC standards. Crunches should be performed explosively, rest interval between each set will be equal to the time it takes to perform the first set of crunches. Rest interval should be assessed each week and adjusted as needed.

Crunches	35	35	35	35	35

3x10

- 30 sec rest between rds
- Banded Explosive Fly's
- TRX Explosive Squats
- DB Curl to Press
- 60 sec rest between rounds

→ SA Farmers Carry x90m switch arms halfway

→ Front Plank x: 45

→ SA Farmers Carry x90m switch arms halfway

→ Left Plank x: 45

→ SA Farmers Carry x90m switch arms halfway

→ Right Plank x: 45

→ SA Farmers Carry x90m switch arms halfway

→ Front Plank x: 45

SESSION 32

OBJECTIVE: STAMINA

These sprints are designed to be max effort sprints. Your rest interval is going to be the average of the time it took you to run your first two 300m sprints. That rest interval will be the same for EVERY sprint. Your rest is a rest in motion, keep the body erect and moving.

If your times begin to vary more than 10%, you need to take additional rest in order to get your timing back within the 10%. However do not exceed the rest interval if not necessary, it is key to progress!

Distance	300m	300m	300m	300m
Time				

Distance	200m	200m	200m	200m	200m	200m	200m	200m	200m	200m
Time										

Distance	100m	100m	100m	100m	100m	100m	100m	100m
Time								

SESSION 33

OBJECTIVE: STRENGTH

- → **Deadlift - 4x10 - 90 sec Rest Between RDS**
- → **DB Pullover - 4x10 - 90 sec Rest Between RDS**
- → **DB Bent Over row - 4x10 - 90 sec Rest Between RDS**

Pull Ups Should be performed in accordance with USMC standards. If you are unable to perform the prescribed pull ups, the remainder can be assisted with bands. Rest interval should be equal to the amount of time it takes to perform the first set of pull-ups. Perform each rep as quickly and as explosively as possible.

Pull Ups	11	10	8	4	4

3x10

- 30 sec rest between rds
- DB front raise
- DB lateral raise
- Rest 45 sec between rounds

3x10

- 30 sec rest between rds
- TRX Glute bridge w row
- TRX pike
- Rest 60 sec between rounds

4 rounds

- Ball Snatch to Slam
- : 20-sec on
- : 20-sec off

SESSION 34

OBJECTIVE: POOL PT

Push Ups should be performed to USMC standards.

Rest interval between each set of push ups will be the amount of time in sec it took to perform 22 push ups. Assess this time each week and adjust accordingly.

Push Up	22	22	20	18	18	10	10	8	8

Stroke refinement and skills acquisition

Some iterations will be performed wearing Swim Trunks and some with cammie tops & bottoms. Ensure you check the prescribed attire.

Rest iteration between prescribed tasks are to be no more than 5 mins. By this point you should be comfortable with full cammies.

Swim sessions should always be performed in the presence of a lifeguard or another individual who is able to provide assistance if necessary.

Swim Trunks

- Side Stroke Left Side - 4x25m
- Side Stroke Right Side - 4x25m
- Breast Stroke - 4x25m

Cammie Top & Bottoms

- Side Stroke Left Side - 2x25m
- Side Stroke Right Side - 2x25m
- Breast Stroke - 2x25m

Underwater Crossover

- Cammie Top & Bottoms - 3x10m
- Swim Trunks - 2x15m

Tread Water

- Cammie Top & Bottoms - 2x 5 mins
- Swim Trunks - 2x 10 mins

SESSION 35

OBJECTIVE: STRENGTH

4 rounds

- 25M-Down & Back x6= 300m
- 1:30 rest

Plate rack hold walking lunges- 4x10 - 90 sec Rest Between RDS

→ DB floor press - 4x10 - 90 sec Rest Between RDS

→ Cuban Press - 4x10 - 90 sec Rest Between RDS

→ DB bent over row - 4x10 - 90 sec Rest Between RDS

→ Band retractions - 4x10 - 90 sec Rest Between RDS

Crunches should be performed to USMC standards. Crunches should be performed explosively, rest interval between each set will be equal to the time it takes to perform the first set of crunches. Rest interval should be assessed each week and adjusted as needed.

Crunches	35	35	35	35	35

Pull Ups Should be performed in accordance with USMC standards. If you are unable to perform the prescribed pull ups, the remainder can be assisted with bands. Rest interval should be equal to the amount of time it takes to perform the first set of pullups. Perform each rep as quickly and as explosively as possible.

Pull Ups	11	10	8	4	4

3x12

- 20 sec rest between exercises
- TRX Side Crunch
- KB Alt lateral Lunge
- Rest 45 sec between rounds

3x12

- 20 sec rest between exercises
- MB Side Throws
- Bar Hang knee raise
- Alternating Jump Lunge
- Rest 60 sec between rounds

SESSION 36

OBJECTIVE: ACTIVE RECOVERY DAYS:

1 Hour Sustained Activity. You can Hike, Run, Swim, Bike, Row or Play Football, Rugby, Soccer, Basketball. Any activity of your choice where you have sustained movement for a minimum of 1 hour.

Record Steps/Distance each week.

WEEK 7

SESSION 37

OBJECTIVE: STRENGTH

Shuttle Run

- 5 rounds
- 10/20/30 Down & Back
- : 45-sec rest

→ DKB Rack Squat - 4x8 - 90 sec rest between rounds

→ TRX Bulg Split Squat 4x8 90 sec rest between rounds

→ DB Incline press - 4x8 - 90 sec rest between rounds

→ DB Push Press - 4x8 - 90 sec rest between rounds

Push Ups should be performed to USMC standards.

Rest interval between each set of push ups will be the amount of time in sec it took to perform 22 push-ups. Assess this time each week and adjust accordingly.

Push Up	24	22	20	18	18	10	10	8	8

Crunches should be performed to USMC standards. Crunches should be performed explosively, rest interval between each set will be equal to the time it takes to perform the first set of crunches. Rest interval should be assessed each week and adjusted as needed.

Crunches	35	35	35	35	35

3x10

- 30 sec rest between rds
- Banded Explosive Fly's
- TRX Explosive Squats
- DB Curl to Press
- 60 sec rest between rounds

→ DA Farmer Carry x90m switch arms halfway

→ Front Plank x:45

→ DA Farmer Carry x90m switch arms halfway

→ Left Plank x:45

→ DA Farmer Carry x90m switch arms halfway

→ Right Plank x:45

→ DA Farmer Carry x90m switch arms halfway

→ Front Plank x:45

SESSION 38

OBJECTIVE: STAMINA

These sprints are designed to be max effort sprints. Your rest interval is going to be the average of the time it took you to run your first two 300m sprints. That rest interval will be the same for EVERY sprint. Your rest is a rest in motion; keep the body erect and moving.

If your times begin to vary more than 10%, you need to take additional rest in order to get your timing back within the 10%. However, do not exceed the rest interval if not necessary, it is key to progress!

Distance	300m	300m	300m	300m	300m	300m
Time						

Distance	200m	200m	200m	200m	200m	200m	200m	200m	200m	200m

Time										

Distance	100m	100m	100m	100m	100m	100m	100m	100m	100m	100m
Time										

SESSION 39

OBJECTIVE: STRENGTH

→ **Deadlift - 4x8 - 90 sec rest between rounds**

→ **Lat pulldown - 4x8 - 90 sec rest between rounds**

→ **Seated row - 4x8 - 90 sec rest between rounds**

Pull Ups Should be performed in accordance with USMC standards. If you are unable to perform the prescribed pull ups, the remainder can be assisted with bands. Rest interval should be equal to the amount of time it takes to perform the first set of pullups. Perform each rep as quickly and as explosively as possible.

Pull Ups	6	6	6	5	4

3x10

- 30 sec rest between rds
- DB front raise
- DB lateral raise

3x10

- 30 sec rest between rds
- TRX Glute bridge w/row
- TRX pike
- Rest 60 sec between rounds

5 rounds

- Ball Snatch to Slam
- :20 sec on
- :20 sec off

SESSION 40

OBJECTIVE: POOL PT

Push Ups should be performed to USMC standards.

Rest interval between each set of push ups will be the amount of time in sec it took to perform 22 push-ups. Asses this time each week and adjust accordingly.

Push Up	22	22	20	18	18	10	10	8	8

Stroke refinement and skills acquisition

Some iterations will be performed wearing Swim Trunks and some with cammie tops & bottoms. Ensure you check the prescribed attire.

Rest iteration between prescribed tasks are to be no more than 5 mins.

By this point you should be comfortable with full cammies.

Swim sessions should always be performed in the presence of a lifeguard or another individual who is able to provide assistance if necessary.

Swim Trunks

- Side Stroke Left Side - 3x50m
- Side Stroke Right Side - 3x50m
- Breast Stroke - 3x50m

Underwater Crossover

- Swim Trunks - 4x25m

Tread Water

- Swim Trunks - 2x 15 mins

SESSION 41

OBJECTIVE: STRENGTH

4 rounds

- 25M-Down & Back x6= 300m
- 1:00 rest

→ DKB rack walking lunges - 4x8 - 90 sec rest between rounds

→ Explosive glute bridge - 4x10 - 90 sec rest between rounds

→ BB floor press - 4x8 - 90 sec rest between rounds

→ Alternating SADB row - 4x8 - 90 sec rest between rounds

Crunches should be performed to USMC standards. Crunches should be performed explosively, rest interval between each set will be equal to the time it takes to perform the first set of crunches. Rest interval should be assessed each week and adjusted as needed.

Crunches	35	35	35	35	35

3x12

- 20 sec rest between exercises
- TRX Side Crunch
- KB Alt lateral Lunge
- MB Slams
- Rest 60 sec between rounds

3x12

- 20 sec rest between exercises
- MB Side Throws
- Bar Hang knee raise
- Alternating Jump Lunge

- **Rest 60 sec between rounds**

SESSION 42

OBJECTIVE: ACTIVE RECOVERY DAYS:

1 Hour Sustained Activity. You can Hike, Run, Swim, Bike, Row or Play Football, Rugby, Soccer, Basketball. Any activity of your choice where you have sustained movement for a minimum of 1 hour.

Record Steps/Distance each week.

WEEK 8 (PFT & CFT)

SESSION 43

OBJECTIVE: PFT

This is a MAX effort event for all prescribed components! Leave nothing in the tank. This will get a real full picture as to where you are sitting. **Refer to charts from Requirements for point charts**

PFT	QTY. / TIME	POINTS
CRUNCHES		
PULL-UPS		
3 MILE RUN		

PFT SCORE -

SESSION 44

OBJECTIVE: RECOVERY

This day is designed to be similar to your active recovery days. Perform the daily warm up protocol, stay active but keep the intensity lower. Stay active but remember it is still a recovery day. You should have left nothing on the table on yesterday and are prepping for your CFT in two days.

SESSION 45

OBJECTIVE: RECOVERY

This day is designed to be similar to your active recovery days. Perform the daily warm up protocol, stay active but keep the intensity lower. Stay active but remember it is still a recovery day. You should have left nothing on the table on two days ago and are prepping for your CFT in tomorrow.

SESSION 46

OBJECTIVE: CFT-

This is a MAX effort event for all prescribed components! Leave nothing in the tank. This will get a real full picture as to where you are sitting. **Refer to charts from Requirements for point charts**

CFT	QTY. / TIME	POINT S
AMMO CAN LIFT (ACL)		
MOVEMENT TO CONTACT (MTC)		
MANEUVER UNDER FIRE (MANUF)		

CFT SCORE -

SESSION 47

OBJECTIVE: SWIM

→ Stroke refinement and skills acquisition

→ Ensure you check the prescribed attire.

→ Rest iteration between prescribed tasks are to be no more than 5 mins.

→ By this point you should be comfortable with full cammies.

Swim sessions should always be performed in the presence of a lifeguard or another individual who is able to provide assistance if necessary.

Swim Trunks

- Side Stroke Left Side - 4x25m
- Side Stroke Right Side - 4x25m
- Breast Stroke - 4x25m

Underwater Crossover

- Swim Trunks - 2x25m

Tread Water

- Swim Trunks - 2x 10 mins

SESSION 48

OBJECTIVE: ACTIVE RECOVERY DAYS:

1 Hour Sustained Activity. You can Hike, Run, Swim, Bike, Row or Play Football, Rugby, Soccer, Basketball. Any activity of your choice where you have sustained movement for a minimum of 1 hour.

Record Steps/Distance each week.

WEEK 9

SESSION 49

OBJECTIVE: STRENGTH

Shuttle Run

- 5 rounds
- 10/20/30 Down & Back
- : 40-sec rest

→ DKB Rack Squat - 3x6 - 2 min rest

→ DB Bench - 3x6 - 2 min rest

→ Kneeling Alt DB Press - 3x6 - 2min rest

Crunches should be performed to USMC standards. Crunches should be performed explosively, rest interval between each set will be equal to the time it takes to perform the first set of crunches. Rest interval should be assessed each week and adjusted as needed.

Crunches	35	35	35	35	35

Push Ups should be performed to USMC standards.

Rest interval between each set of push-ups will be the amount of time in sec it took to perform 22 push-ups. Assess this time each week and adjust accordingly.

Push Ups	22	22	20	18	18	8	6

3x12

- TRX High Row
- TRX Bicep Curl
- Rest 60 sec between rounds

3x12

- TRX Triceps Extension
- TRX Pistols
- Rest 60 sec between rounds

3 rounds

- DA Farmer carry - 1:00 min for distance
- DB Push Press x12
- :90-sec rest between sets

SESSION 50

OBJECTIVE: STAMINA

These sprints are designed to be max effort sprints. Your rest interval is going to be the average of the time it took you to run your first two 300m sprints. That rest interval will be the same for EVERY sprint. Your rest is a rest in motion, keep the body erect and moving.

If your times begin to vary more than 10%, you need to take additional rest in order to get your timing back within the 10%. However do not exceed the rest interval if not necessary, it is key to progress!

Distance	300m	300m	300m	300m	300m	300m	300m	300m
Time								

D	200 m	200 m	200 m	200 m	200 m	200 m	200 m	200 m	200 m	200 m	200 m	200 m

T												

D	100m	100m	100m	100m	100m	100m	100m	100m	100m	100m	100m	100m	100m	100m
T														

SESSION 51

OBJECTIVE: STRENGTH

- → **Deadlift - 3x6- 2 min rest**
- → **Lat Pulldown - 3x6- 2 min rest**
- → **Chest Support DB Row - 3x6- 2 min rest**

Pull Ups Should be performed in accordance with USMC standards. If you are unable to perform the prescribed pull ups, the remainder can be assisted with bands. Rest interval should be equal to the amount of time it takes to perform the first set of pullups. Perform each rep as quickly and as explosively as possible.

Pull Ups	6	6	6	5	4

3x10

- 90 sec rest between sets
- DB Front Raise
- Band Press Outs(explosive alternating)
- DB Lateral Raise

3x10

- 90 sec rest between sets
- DB Pull Over
- TRX Glute Bridge with Curl

3x:30sec

- 2 min rest between rounds
- KB Swing
- Bar Hang Knee Raises(explosive)

SESSION 52

OBJECTIVE: POOL PT

Push Ups should be performed to USMC standards.

Rest interval between each set of push ups will be the amount of time in sec it took to perform 22 push-ups. Assess this time each week and adjust accordingly.

Push Ups	22	22	20	18	18	8	6

Stroke refinement and skills acquisition

Some iterations will be performed wearing Swim Trunks and some with cammie tops & bottoms. Ensure you check the prescribed attire.

Rest iteration between prescribed tasks are to be no more than 5 mins. By this point you should be comfortable with full cammies.

Swim sessions should always be performed in the presence of a lifeguard or another individual who is able to provide assistance if necessary.

Swim Trunks

- Side Stroke Left Side - 2x75m
- Side Stroke Right Side - 2x75m
- Breast Stroke - 2x75m

Cammie Bottoms

- Side Stroke Left Side - 2x25m
- Side Stroke Right Side - 2x25m
- Breast Stroke - 2x25m

Underwater Crossover

- Cammie Bottoms - 3x15m
- Swim Trunks - 2x25m

Tread Water

- Cammie Bottoms - 2x 5 mins
- Swim Trunks - 2x 15 mins

SESSION 53

OBJECTIVE: STRENGTH

4 rounds

- 25M-Down & Back x6= 300m
- 1:00 rest

→ DB Step Ups - 3x6 - 2 min rest between sets

→ DB Incline Press - 3x6 - 2 min rest between sets

→ Plyo Push Up - 3x5 2 min rest between sets

→ Seated Row - 3x6 - 2 min rest between sets

Crunches should be performed to USMC standards. Crunches should be performed explosively, rest interval between each set will be equal to the time it takes to perform the first set of crunches. Rest interval should be assessed each week and adjusted as needed.

Crunches	35	35	35	35	35

Pull Ups Should be performed in accordance with USMC standards. If you are unable to perform the prescribed pull ups, the remainder can be assisted with bands. Rest interval should be equal to the amount of time it takes to perform the first set of pullups. Perform each rep as quickly and as explosively as possible.

Pull Ups	6	6	6	5	4

3x12

- 90 sec rest between sets
- Power step Ups
- Band Rotations

3x12

- 90 sec rest between sets
- TRX Explosive Squats
- TRX Face Pull

4x: 30-sec

- Plate Pinch Carry
- TRX Plank alternate F/R/L/F

SESSION 54

OBJECTIVE: ACTIVE RECOVERY DAYS:

1 Hour Sustained Activity. You can Hike, Run, Swim, Bike, Row or Play Football, Rugby, Soccer, Basketball. Any activity of your choice where you have sustained movement for a minimum of 1 hour.

Record Steps/Distance each week.

WEEK 10

SESSION 55

OBJECTIVE: STRENGTH

Shuttle Run

- 5 rounds
- 10/20/30 Down & Back
- : 35-sec rest

→ Goblet Squat - 3x5 - Max 2 min rest

→ Explosive Jump - 3x5 Max 2 min rest

→ DB Floor Press - 3x5 - Max 2 min rest

→ Cuban Press - 3x5 Max 2 min rest

→ Standing Alt Db Press - 3x5 - Max 2 min rest

Crunches should be performed to USMC standards. Crunches should be performed explosively, rest interval between each set will be equal to the time it takes to perform the first set of crunches. Rest interval should be assessed each week and adjusted as needed.

Crunches	35	35	35	35	35

Push Ups should be performed to USMC standards.

Rest interval between each set of push-ups will be the amount of time in sec it took to perform 22 push-ups. Assess this time each week and adjust accordingly.

Push Ups	22	22	20	18	18	10	10

3x10

- 60 sec rest between rounds
- TRX Push Up w/Pike
- DB Hammer Curl to Press

3x10

- 60 sec rest between rounds
- TRX Tricep Extension
- TRX Pistols

4 rounds

- Uneven weight farmer carry - 1:00 min for distance
- DB Chest Press x10
- : 90-sec rest between sets

SESSION 56

OBJECTIVE: STAMINA

These sprints are designed to be max effort sprints. Your rest interval is going to be the average of the time it took you to run your first two 300m sprints. That rest interval will be the same for EVERY sprint. Your rest is a rest in motion, keep the body erect and moving.

If your times begin to vary more than 10%, you need to take additional rest in order to get your timing back within the 10%. However do not exceed the rest interval if not necessary, it is key to progress!

Distance	300m	300m	300m	300m	300m	300m	300m	300m
Time								

D	200m	200m	200m	200m	200m	200m	200m	200m	200m	200m	200m	200m

Time												

D	100 m	100 m	100 m	100 m	100 m	100 m	100 m	100 m	100 m	100 m	100 m	100 m	100 m	100 m
T														

SESSION 57

OBJECTIVE: STRENGTH

- → **Deadlift - 3x5 - Max 2 min rest**
- → **Band Pull Throughs - 3x8 Max 2 min rest**
- → **Lat Pulldown - 3x5 - Max 2 min rest**
- → **DB Bent over Row - 3x5 - Max 2 min rest**

Pull Ups Should be performed in accordance with USMC standards. If you are unable to perform the prescribed pull ups, the remainder can be assisted with bands. Rest interval should be equal to the amount of time it takes to perform the first set of pullups. Perform each rep as quickly and as explosively as possible.

Pull Ups	7	6	5	4	4	4

3x10

- 90 sec rest between sets
- DB Front Raise
- Band Press Outs(explosive alternating)
- DB Lateral Raise

3x10

- 90 sec rest between sets
- Explosive Band Retractions
- TRX Glute Bridge with Curl

3x:30sec

- 2 min rest between rounds
- KB Swing
- Bar Hang Knee Raises(explosive)

SESSION 58

OBJECTIVE: POOL PT

Push Ups should be performed to USMC standards.

Rest interval between each set of push-ups will be the amount of time in sec it took to perform 22 push-ups. Assess this time each week and adjust accordingly.

Push Ups	22	22	20	18	18	10	10

Some iterations will be performed wearing Swim Trunks and some with cammie tops & bottoms. Ensure you check the prescribed attire.

Rest iteration between prescribed tasks are to be no more than 5 mins.

By this point you should be comfortable with full cammies.

***Swim sessions should always be performed in the presence of a lifeguard or another individual who is able to provide assistance if neccessary. ***

Swim Trunks

- Side Stroke Left Side - 1x150m
- Side Stroke Right Side - 1x150m
- Breast Stroke - 1x150m

Cammie Bottoms

- Side Stroke Left Side - 2x25m
- Side Stroke Right Side - 2x25m
- Breast Stroke - 2x25m

Underwater Crossover

- Cammie Bottoms - 3x15m
- Swim Trunks - 2x25m

Tread Water

- Cammie Bottoms - 2x 5 mins
- Swim Trunks - 2x 15 mins

SESSION 59

OBJECTIVE: STRENGTH

4 rounds

- 25M-Down & Back x6= 300m
- 1:00 rest

→ Double KB Rack Walking Lunges - 3x5 each leg - Max 2 min rest

→ Alternating DB Incline Press - 3x5 - Max 2 min rest

→ Banded Flys - 3x8 Max 2 min rest

→ Single Arm DB Row - 3x5 - Max 2 min rest

Crunches should be performed to USMC standards. Crunches should be performed explosively, rest interval between each set will be equal to the time it takes to perform the first set of crunches. Rest interval should be assessed each week and adjusted as needed.

Crunches	35	35	35	35	35

Pull Ups Should be performed in accordance with USMC standards. If you are unable to perform the prescribed pull ups, the remainder can be assisted with bands. Rest interval should be equal to the amount of time it takes to perform the first set of pullups. Perform each rep as quickly and as explosively aspossible.

Pull Ups	7	6	5	4	4	4

3x10

- 90 sec rest between sets
- TRX Alternating Lateral Lunge
- DB Curls

3x10

- 90 sec rest between sets
- TRX Push Up with Pike
- TRX Bulgarian Split Squat

3x:30sec

- 2 min rest between rounds
- Plate Farmer Carry
- Wall Sit

SESSION 60

OBJECTIVE: ACTIVE RECOVERY DAYS:

1 Hour Sustained Activity. You can Hike, Run, Swim, Bike, Row or Play Football, Rugby, Soccer, Basketball. Any activity of your choice where you have sustained movement for a minimum of 1 hour.

Record Steps/Distance each week.

WEEK 11

SESSION 61

OBJECTIVE: STRENGTH

Shuttle Run

- 5 rounds
- 10/20/30 Down & Back
- : 30-sec rest

→ DKB Rack Squat - 4x4 - 2 min rest between sets

→ DB Bench - 4x4 - 2 min rest between sets

→ DB Chest Press - 4x4 - 2min rest between sets

5Push Ups should be performed to USMC standards.

Rest interval between each set of push-ups will be the amount of time in sec it took to perform 22 pushups. Assess this time each week and adjust accordingly.

Push Ups	22	22	20	18	18	10	10	10

Crunches should be performed to USMC standards. Crunches should be performed explosively; rest interval between each set will be equal to the time it takes to perform the first set of crunches. Rest interval should be assessed each week and adjusted as needed.

Crunches	35	35	35	35	35

3x10

- 90 sec rest between rounds
- TRX Explosive Squats
- TRX Bicep Curl

3x10

- 90 sec rest between rounds
- TRX Tricep Extension
- TRX Pistols

3 rounds

- Farmers carry - :45 min for distance
- Standing Alternating DB Press x8
- : 90-sec rest between sets

SESSION 62

OBJECTIVE: STAMINA

These sprints are designed to be max effort sprints. Your rest interval is going to be the average of the time it took you to run your first two 300m sprints. That rest interval will be the same for EVERY sprint. Your rest is a rest in motion, keep the body erect and moving.

If your times begin to vary more than 10%, you need to take additional rest in order to get your timing back within the 10%. However, do not exceed the rest interval if not necessary, it is key to progress!

Distance	300m	300m	300m	300m
Time				

Distance	200m	200m	200m	200m	200m	200m	200m	200m
Time								

Distance	100m	100m	100m	100m	100m	100m	100m	100m
Time								

SESSION 63

OBJECTIVE: STRENGTH

- → Deadlift - 4x4- Max 2 min rest
- → Vertical Jump - 4x4 Max 2 min rest
- → Lat Pulldown - 4x4- Max 2 min rest
- → Band Explosive Pull Down - 4x4 each arm Max 2 min rest
- → SADB Row - 4x4- Max 2 min rest

Pull Ups Should be performed in accordance with USMC standards. If you are unable to perform the prescribed pull ups, the remainder can be assisted with bands. Rest interval should be equal to the amount of time it takes to perform the first set of pull-ups. Perform each rep as quickly and as explosively as possible.

Pull Ups	8	7	6	4	4	3

SESSION 64

OBJECTIVE: POOL PT

Push Ups should be performed to USMC standards.

Rest interval between each set of push-ups will be the amount of time in sec it took to perform 22 push-ups. Assess this time each week and adjust accordingly.

Push Ups	22	22	20	18	18	10	10	10

Some iterations will be performed wearing Swim Trunks and some with cammie tops & bottoms. Ensure you check the prescribed attire.

Rest iteration between prescribed tasks are to be no more than 5 mins. By this point you should be comfortable with full cammies.

Swim sessions should always be performed in the presence of a lifeguard or another individual who is able to provide assistance if necessary.

Swim Trunks

- Side Stroke Left Side - 1x200m
- Side Stroke Right Side - 1x200m
- Breast Stroke - 1x200m

Cammie Top & Bottoms

- Side Stroke Left Side - 2x25m
- Side Stroke Right Side - 2x25m
- Breast Stroke - 2x25m

Underwater Crossover

- Cammie Top & Bottoms - 3x15m
- Swim Trunks - 3x25m

Tread Water

- No stopping between uniform change
- Cammie Top & Bottoms- 10min - Strip Top/Just Bottoms- 10mins - Strip Bottoms/Trunks-10mins

SESSION 65

OBJECTIVE: STRENGTH

4 rounds

- 25M-Down & Back x6= 300m
- 1:00 rest

→ DB Step Ups - 4x4 - Max 2 min rest

→ DB Incline Press - 4x4 - Max 2 min rest

→ Elevated Push Up - 4x5 Max 2 min rest

→ DB Bent Over Row - 4x4 - Max 2 min rest

Crunches should be performed to USMC standards. Crunches should be performed explosively, rest interval between each set will be equal to the time it takes to perform the first set of crunches. Rest interval should be assessed each week and adjusted as needed.

Crunches	35	35	35	35	35

Pull Ups Should be performed in accordance with USMC standards. If you are unable to perform the prescribed pull ups, the remainder can be assisted with bands. Rest interval should be equal to the amount of time it takes to perform the first set of pullups. Perform each rep as quickly and as explosively aspossible.

Pull Ups	8	7	6	4	4	3

3x12

- 90 sec rest between sets
- Power step Ups
- Band Rotations

3x12

- 90 sec rest between sets
- TRX Explosive Squats
- TRX Face Pull

4x:30sec

- Plate Pinch Carry
- TRX Plank alternate F/R/L/F

SESSION 66

OBJECTIVE: ACTIVE RECOVERY DAYS:

1 Hour Sustained Activity. You can Hike, Run, Swim, Bike, Row or Play Football, Rugby, Soccer, Basketball. Any activity of your choice where you have sustained movement for a minimum of 1 hour.

Record Steps/Distance each week.

WEEK 12

SESSION 67

OBJECTIVE: STRENGTH

Shuttle Run

- 5 rounds
- 10/20/30 Down & Back
- :45 sec rest

Goblet Squat - 4x3

- Explosive Jump - 4x5
- 2 min rest between rounds

DB Floor Press - 4x3

- Cuban Press - 4x5
- 2 min rest between rounds

Standing Alt DB Press - 4x3

- 2 min rest between rounds

Push Ups should be performed to USMC standards.

Rest interval between each set of push-ups will be the amount of time in sec it took to perform 22 push-ups. Assess this time each week and adjust accordingly.

Push Ups	22	22	20	18	18	10

3x8

- 90 sec rest between rounds
- TRX Push Up w/Pike
- DB Hammer Curl to Press

3x8

- 90 sec rest between rounds
- TRX Tricep Extension
- TRX Pistols

3 rounds

- Uneven weight farmer carry - 1:00 for max distance (switch hands/weight halfway)
- DB Chest Press x8
- :90 sec rest between sets

SESSION 68

OBJECTIVE: STAMINA

These sprints are designed to be max effort sprints. Your rest interval is going to be the average of the time it took you to run your first two 300m sprints. That rest interval will be the same for EVERY sprint. Your rest is a rest in motion, keep the body erect and moving.

If your times begin to vary more than 10%, you need to take additional rest in order to get your timing back within the 10%. However do not exceed the rest interval if not necessary, it is key to progress!

Distance	300m	300m

Distance	200m	200m	200m	200m	200m	200m

Time						

Distance	100m	100m	100m	100m	100m	100m
Time						

SESSION 69

OBJECTIVE: STRENGTH

Deadlift - 4x3- 2 min rest

- Broad Jump - 4x4
- 2 min rest between rounds

Lat Pull Down - 4x3

- Band Explosive Pull Down - 4x4 each arm
- 2 min rest between rounds

Single Arm DB Row - 4x3

- 2 min rest between rounds

Crunches should be performed to USMC standards. Crunches should be performed explosively, rest interval between each set will be equal to the time it takes to perform the first set of crunches. Rest interval should be assessed each week and adjusted as needed.

Crunches	35	35	35	35	35

Pull Ups Should be performed in accordance with USMC standards. If you are unable to perform the prescribed pull ups, the remainder can be assisted with bands. Rest interval should be equal to the amount of time it takes to perform the first set of pullups. Perform each rep as quickly and as explosively as possible.

Pull Ups	9	8	6	4	3	3

3x8

- 90 sec rest between sets
- DB Front Raise
- Band Press Outs (explosive alternating)
- DB Lateral Raise

3x8

- 90 sec rest between sets
- Explosive Band Retractions
- TRX Glute Bridge with hello dolly

3x: 20-sec

- 2 min rest between rounds
- KB Swing
- Bar Hang Knee Raises(explosive)

SESSION 70

OBJECTIVE: POOL PT

Push Ups should be performed to USMC standards.

Rest interval between each set of push-ups will be the amount of time in sec it took to perform 22 push-ups. Assess this time each week and adjust accordingly.

Push Ups	22	22	20	18	18	10

Some iterations will be performed wearing Swim Trunks and some with cammie tops & bottoms. Ensure you check the prescribed attire.

Rest iteration between prescribed tasks are to be no more than 5 mins. By this point you should be comfortable with full cammies.

Swim sessions should always be performed in the presence of a lifeguard or another individual who is able to provide assistance if necessary.

Swim Trunks

- Side Stroke Left Side - 2x50m
- Side Stroke Right Side - 2x50m
- Breast Stroke - 2x50m

Cammie Top & Bottoms

- Side Stroke Left Side - 2x25m
- Side Stroke Right Side - 2x25m
- Breast Stroke - 2x25m

Underwater Crossover

- Cammie Top & Bottoms - 3x15m
- Swim Trunks - 3x25m

Tread Water

- No stopping between uniform change
- Cammie Top & Bottoms- 10min - Strip Top/Just Bottoms- 10mins - Strip Bottoms/Trunks-10mins

SESSION 71

OBJECTIVE: STRENGTH

Shuttle Run

- 4 rounds
- 10/20/30 Down & Back
- : 45-sec rest

DKB Rack Walking Lunges - 3x5 each leg

- 2min rest between rounds

Alternating DB Incline Press - 3x5

- Banded Flys - 3x8
- 2 min rest between rounds

→ SADB Row - 3x5 - 2min rest between rounds

Crunches should be performed to USMC standards. Crunches should be performed explosively, rest interval between each set will be equal to the time it takes to perform the first set of crunches. Rest interval should be assessed each week and adjusted as needed.

Crunches	35	35	35	35	35

Pull Ups Should be performed in accordance with USMC standards. If you are unable to perform the prescribed pull ups, the remainder can be assisted with bands. Rest interval should be equal to the amount of time it takes to perform the first set of pullups. Perform each rep as quickly and as explosively as possible.

Pull Ups	7	6	5	4	4	4

3x8

- 90 sec rest between sets
- TRX Alternating Lateral Lunge
- DB Curls

3x8

- 90 sec rest between sets
- TRX Push Up with Pike
- TRX Bulgarian Split Squat

3x: 20-sec

- 2 min rest between rounds
- Plate Farmer Carry
- Wall Sit

SESSION 72

OBJECTIVE: ACTIVE RECOVERY DAYS:

1 Hour Sustained Activity. You can Hike, Run, Swim, Bike, Row or Play Football, Rugby, Soccer, Basketball. Any activity of your choice where you have sustained movement for a minimum of 1 hour.

Record Steps/Distance each week.

CONGRATULATIONS!

You have just completed 12 weeks of USMC PREP. If you are now leaving for Recruit training then Josh and Nick wish you good luck and want to hear from you on the other side. If you have some more time, then they want you to start this program over from the beginning. Even though it is the same, you will have improved your body mechanics, stability, performance, repetitions, weight, and times. This will now be a new starting base to apply the protocol. Take off one full week and then begin another 12-week cycle. If time is not on your side take one week off, during that week perform mobility, stability, and body weight/ active recovery. Upon completion of that week, perform a Marine Corps. PFT on Monday and a CFT on Thursday.

Annotate your scores below.

This is a MAX effort event for all prescribed components! Leave nothing in the tank. This will get a real full picture as to where you are sitting.

PFT	QTY. / TIME	POINTS
CRUNCHES		
PULL-UPS		
3 MILE RUN		

PFT SCORE -

This is a MAX effort event for all prescribed components! Leave nothing in the tank. This will get a real full picture as to where you are sitting.

CFT	QTY. / TIME	POINTS
AMMO CAN LIFT (ACL)		
MOVEMENT TO CONTACT (MTC)		
MANEUVER UNDER FIRE (MANUF)		

CFT SCORE -

THE AUTHORS

NICK KOUMALATSOS

Nick spent 12 years in the United States Marine Corps. He graduated Marine Basic Training as Company Honor Man. He went on to serve with 2D Force Recon Co and 3rd Reconnaissance Bn. His last 5 years was spent with Marine Special Operations Command at 2D Raider Bn as a Marine Raider.

JOSH HONSBERGER

Josh spent 13 years in the United States Marine Corps. He spent his first 5 years grinding it as a Marine Infantryman. He then transferred to Quantico to as an instructor/trainer Foreign Weapons, High Risk Personal, and Small Arms weapons Instructor Course. His last 5 years was spent with Marine Special Operations Command at 2D Raider Bn as a Marine Raider.

As always, let Josh and Nick know if there are any issues.

Never Quit, Never Surrender, Always Forward!

Want to e-mail Nick? Nick@alexanderind.com

Want to e-mail Josh? Josh@alexanderind.com

Made in the USA
Lexington, KY
25 June 2019